How to Settle Debts Yourself

by Sandee Ferman

Copyright, Legal Notice and Disclaimer:

Table of Contents

Why Read This Book?.. 1

Chapter One – Your Debts... 3

List every debt owed, no matter how old or small ... 4

Budget.. 8
Income 8
Expenses.. 12

Evaluate income versus expenses......................... 17
Do you have more money coming in than going
out? How much?... 17

Chapter Two – Your Options 19

Option One: Pay it 19
Cut down on expenses, and pay the debts 19
Increase your income, and pay the debts........... 21
How to pay off your debts faster 21
Get a loan to pay your debts 24
Contact your creditors and get them to extend the
loan, or lower the interest rate, or work out a
payment plan so you can pay off the debts........ 26

Option Two: Debt Management Plan (Credit Counseling) 29

Option Three: Debt Settlement 32

Option Four: Bankruptcy 33

Bankruptcy Chapter 7 (eliminates all debts except some secured debts, varies by state) 33
Bankruptcy Chapter 11 (mostly for businesses) . 34
Bankruptcy Chapter 13 (repayment plan mandated by courts) 35

Option Five: Walk away from the debt 37

Verification of Debt 44

Chapter Three – Your Decision 47

Scenario: Single, young, with student loans and credit card debts 48
Scenario: Middle-aged, divorced, credit card debts with high interest rates 49
Scenario: Over your head in debts and cannot meet minimum payments 50
Scenario: Owe more than you own and can never pay it all back 51
Scenario: Not sure if you should choose Debt Management or Debt Settlement 52

Chapter Four - Settle it yourself 53

First Step: Contact Your Creditors.......................... 53

A Sample Conversation with Your Creditor 59

Some buzzwords you'll want to remember............ 63

    Hardship 63
    Bankruptcy 64
    Insolvency.. 65
    Charge off.. 65
    Statute of Limitations 67
    Original creditor.. 68
    Collection agency.. 69
    FCRA 70
    FDCPA 71

Legal threats... 75

Procedures in your jurisdiction for service of process, and how to respond. 76

    Garnishment... 77
    Lien.. 78
    Levy 78
    Stipulated Judgment 79

Summary of initial contact..................................... 80

Next Step: How to negotiate a settlement............. 82

Settlement "nuts and bolts" – How to get it DONE 88

Start saving money to have available for settling accounts. 89

Where can you keep your money while you are saving? 90

Continue until you are done settling all accounts .. 92

Finally: What is a good settlement offer? 93

Settlement Percentages – the Good, the Bad, the Ugly 95

When is a good time to settle debts? 96

Will I owe taxes on the settlement? 99

Chapter Five - I got sued! 101

It's not a crime to get sued. 101

Do you have assets? 102

Do you have wages? 102

Can your wages be garnished? 102

Do you owe money to the government? 103

Do you want to hire a lawyer or get legal assistance? 103

Do you feel comfortable telling a judge your side of the story? 104

Can you attend the court case? 104

Can you settle the amount due now? 105

What happens if you lose the case? 105

Social Security payments are specially protected. 106

Chapter Six - How do I know I won't get into debt again? 109

    Overspending 109

    Medical Issues 110

    Family Issues.. 111

    Work Issues 112

    Where to find help? 113

    What about purchases? 114

    Take pride in your debt-free status. 114

    Daily expenses 114

Chapter Seven - CONGRATULATIONS! You did it! 115

APPENDIX 117

    Creditor Conversation Follow-Up Letter Explaining Hardship 120

    Creditor Conversation Follow-Up Letter With Written Settlement Offer Request 121

    Settlement Letter Offer (sent from your creditor to you) 122

    Verification of Debt Letter 123

    Hardship Letter... 124

    List of All Debts... 125

    Budget – Income and Expenses – Monthly....... 127

    Statute of Limitations 133

GLOSSARY.. 137

Bankruptcy 137
Bankruptcy Chapter 7 (eliminates all debts except some secured debts, varies by state) 137
Bankruptcy Chapter 11 (mostly for businesses) 138
Bankruptcy Chapter 13 (repayment plan mandated by courts) 138
Charge-off 139
Collection agency 140
Consolidation loan 140
Debt management plan (credit counseling) 140
Debt settlement (debtnegotiation) 141
FCRA 141
FDCPA 141
Garnishment 142
Hardship 142
Insolvency 143
Levy 143
Lien 143
Original creditor 144
Statute of Limitations 144
Stipulated judgment 144
Tools Site 145
Website 146

Acknowledgments 147

About the Author 149

Why Read This Book?

If you have debts and don't know how you'll get rid of them, *this book is for you ...*

If creditors are calling you day and night to collect from you, and you don't have a solution, *this book is for you ...*

If you've wondered how long you'll pay minimum payments, and if you'll ever get out of debt, *this book is for you ...*

If bankruptcy is starting to look like your only choice, *this book is for you ...*

If you'd like to settle your debts, and wonder if you can do it yourself, ***this book is for you!***

Inside you'll find out how to work out a budget; how to figure out what your choices are, and decide on your best choice; you'll get instructions on how to talk to your creditors; you'll get negotiation insights that will help you get your best settlements with your creditors; you'll even receive information about what to do in case you receive a lawsuit from one of your creditors (yes, that can happen, and you need to be prepared so you know what to do).

Many people have debts and need help. You might think you need to get a professional to help you negotiate with your creditors. You don't! I owned a debt settlement company for years and I know most people can do this themselves. If you think you can, this book will show you how to settle your debts yourself.[1]

I don't hold back any secrets. Debt settlement is not that complicated.

You can do it!

This book will show you how. Let's get started.

_____

[1] There is also a glossary for commonly used terms you will need to negotiate better settlements for yourself! Some terms are defined within the book when they are first used. See the glossary when you want to be reminded of their meanings.

Chapter One – Your Debts

How much debt do you owe?

Who do you owe?

What's the total owed to everyone?

Can you locate all the bills you have?

The first step for resolving your debt is locating every debt you owe. This chapter will guide you through that process. You can access tools through my book website **www.HowToSettleDebtsYourself.com** that will perform these calculations for you as you enter the numbers.[2]

---

[2] See the Appendix for more information on these tools, sample forms you can use, and access to our special Tools Site for book purchasers.

List every debt owed, no matter how old or small

On my website I have a form you can use to list all your debts. Save the form to your computer (no information will be stored on my website) and update it as often as you need. In the **List All Debts** form, list the date of debt, the description (name and account number), monthly payment, and total owed right now. There is a column to record notes about the debt, such as "high interest rate" or "interest only" or "they're calling at work" or anything else you'd like to mention. List each debt you have. For the date of debt, you may either use the date you first started having that debt, or the date of the last statement. It's your choice. I prefer to list the date that debt started, so I can see how old the debts are; it gives me more incentive to pay off older debts when I see how long I've had them hanging around.

If you are not using the form from my website, you will need a sheet of paper to list every debt you owe. Be sure to note the account numbers – you will use this list when you contact your creditors. You can also use a spreadsheet to list all the debts and update it as you receive bills each month.

Put all the bills into a folder to keep them organized. You'll want to have a place to record notes for each creditor you contact, and keeping everything in a folder will make it faster to find the files.

Be sure to list EVERYTHING. For example, here are some debts that might be owed:

- Chase VISA card ending in 1843, balance $2,345.90
- Sears card ending in 9870, balance $1,518.99
- Bill from Dr. Smith, balance $295.00
- Loan from Susan, balance $150.00
- Retirement plan loan, balance $2,500.00
- IRS debt, balance $968.05
- Landlord for the apartment I lived in three years ago and didn't pay, balance $345.00
- Ford Motor Credit for the repossessed truck, balance $11,259.11
- Personally guaranteed debt owed to vendor from failed business, balance $23,988.45

Any debt you owe anywhere should be listed here. Be sure to list personally guaranteed debts from businesses that defaulted and you're being held liable for the debt. List unpaid bills from doctors, veterinary, closed timeshares, repossessed vehicles or boats, everything you can think of.

You might not be able to settle all of these debts but most of them should be negotiable. For example, this book will not tell you how to negotiate "loan from Susan" or "IRS debt" but you may be able to use these techniques to work out something after you've worked on the rest. Also, if you have borrowed money from your retirement plan at work, you'll be obligated to pay that debt (most likely from your paycheck) so this book won't be telling you how to settle that debt. You could decide to take that as an early distribution and pay the IRS penalty and taxes but that is a decision you might choose at any time, regardless of the way you take care of any other debts you owe.

Here is an example of the form to list all debts:

Date of Debt	Description of Debt	Monthly Payment	Total Due	Notes

Date of Debt	Description of Debt	Monthly Payment	Total Due	Notes
	Totals			

If you remember other debts later on, add them to this list. If you are using the *List All Debts* form from my website, enter each debt on a new line and the totals will be updated.[3]

All right, now that you have a list of all the debts you can find, let's move on to another topic: your budget.

---

[3] See the Appendix for your username and password to the website tools mentioned throughout this book.

Budget

In a perfect world, you would determine your budget by deciding how much of your monthly income you will be spending on what types of expenses. You would be choosing what to buy, when you want to buy it, and know where the money will be coming from to buy that item or service.

Income

To get started, however, let's first figure out how much income you have coming in each month, or week, or year.

List all income sources, no matter how infrequent. You need to convert the income to a monthly amount – this is how you can do it:

- If the amount is paid monthly, list the full amount.
- If the amount is paid weekly, either multiply by 4.33 to get a monthly amount; or multiply by 52 and divide by 12 to find the monthly amount.
- If the amount is paid yearly, divide by 12.
- If it is paid twice a month, multiply by 2.

- If the amount is paid every two weeks, either multiply by 2.17; or, multiply the income by 26 and divide by 12 to get the monthly income.
- If the amount is paid every three months, divide by 3.
- If the amount is paid every four months, divide by 4.
- If the amount is paid every six months, divide by 6 to find out one month's amount.
- If the amount is paid every day, multiply by 30 (even though some months have 31 days, February has only 28 or 29, so use 30).
- If you are paid with some other frequency, figure out the monthly average and enter that.

Bottom line: you want to list only MONTHLY amounts for all your income sources, even if that monthly amount is an average of a yearly amount. Your goal is to get a pretty close estimate of the amount of income you receive on a monthly basis. Later we will do the same with expenses.[4]

Also, on my website is a **Budget** form you can download and save to your computer, where you can enter your information and keep it updated – as your

---

[4] Don't include the taxes you paid, only use take-home pay when you are calculating your income. List the money you can spend.

information changes, you get another job, or a bill is paid, your budget can change.

If you are not using the form from my website **www.HowToSettleDebtsYourself.com**, write all your income sources on a piece of paper and total them for your monthly income. You can also use a spreadsheet to list all of them. You'll need this list later when it's time to settle your debts with your creditors.

Here are some examples of income sources.

Income Sources	Monthly Amount	How Often is Income Received? *(daily, weekly, monthly, annually)*
Wages or Salary		
Overtime		
Commissions		
Tips		
Bonus		
Social Security, Retirement or Pension		

Income Sources	Monthly Amount	How Often is Income Received? *(daily, weekly, monthly, annually)*
Child Support		
Alimony		
Family Income (from relatives, for example)		
Rental Property		
Insurance Settlement		
Yard Sales		
Tax Refunds		
Trust or Annuity		
Birthday Money		
Holiday Money		
Lottery Winnings		
Other Income		

Income Sources	Monthly Amount	How Often is Income Received? *(daily, weekly, monthly, annually)*
Total Income		

Expenses

Now that you've found every source of income you can, take a look at all your expenses. There is a list on my website at **www.HowToSettleDebtsYourself.com** where you can enter this information and print a copy for your files. By purchasing this book you will have access to a downloadable *Budget* form you can save on your computer, and it will total the expenses as you enter them.

List all expenses. You'll want to list everything you spend money on each month, even if later you decide you don't need it or won't keep spending it. Right now, all we want to do is list ALL the money you spend, so we can see how much money is going out compared with what is coming in, and you can see if there is any extra money available to resolve your debts.

List all debts and all loan payments. List all your credit cards, and all other unsecured loans. An "unsecured loan" means it's not tied to your house, or car, or any other item that can be taken away if you don't pay the loan. For example, utilities are NOT unsecured debts because they can be turned off if you don't pay. However, if you had a car, and didn't pay, and it was repossessed, then any amount you still owe IS an unsecured debt because there's nothing to take away if you don't pay the balance due.

If some expenses are not paid monthly, convert them to monthly amounts before you list them. Use the calculators in the previous income section to adjust them to a monthly expense amount and list that.

Here are some examples of expenses. All are included on my website **www.HowToSettleDebtsYourself.com** in the downloadable *Budget* form, and in the Appendix.

If you are not using the *Budget* form from my website, write these on a piece of paper and total them for your monthly expenses. You can also use a spreadsheet to record them and have them added for you. You'll need this list when it's time to settle your debts with your creditors.

Expenses	Monthly Amount	How Often is Expense Paid?
Rent		
Mortgage		
Child Support		
Alimony		
Vehicle Loans		
Credit Card Payments		
Credit Union Loans		
Groceries		
Dining Out		
School Lunches		
Coffee Cafe		
School Tuition		
Education Loans		

Expenses	Monthly Amount	How Often is Expense Paid?
Charity		
Vehicle Insurance		
Home Insurance		
Life Insurance		
Health Insurance		
Clothing		
Uniforms		
Laundry, Dry Cleaning		
Gasoline		
Telephone, Cell Phones		
Internet		
Cable TV		
Gas, Oil, Coal		

Expenses	Monthly Amount	How Often is Expense Paid?
Electric		
Water		
Sewer, Septic		
Trash		
Other Utilities		
Doctors		
Pharmacy		
Veterinary		
Legal Fees		
Entertainment		
Other Expenses		
Total Expenses		

Evaluate income versus expenses

This is simple if you're using my website's **Budget** form because the balance is calculated as you enter amounts in the Income or Expense sections of the **Budget** form.

The final step is to take your total income and subtract your total expenses, and see what's left. Write down the amount, and make a note if it's extra money or extra expenses. Could be either one, so just make a note and move to the next step.

Income minus Expenses	

Do you have more money coming in than going out? How much?

This is where you finish the assessment. Look over your monthly income and expense lists, make sure you've listed every source of income and every expense you can think of, and take a look at the situation. Are you making more money than you're spending? Or are you spending more money than you're making?

Let's take a look at your options in the next chapter.

Chapter Two – Your Options

Now that you've calculated your income versus expenses, we can take a look at what to do with your debts. Pay them in full? Consolidate them? Seek credit counseling? Settle your debts for a lower payment? File bankruptcy? Walk away from the debts?

Let's take a look at each of these options in more detail and understand the consequences of each one.

Option One: Pay it

In this section you consider the idea of paying all the debts in full. How can you do that? Here are some ideas:

Cut down on expenses, and pay the debts

Here is where your budget information will be used. You have the total income and total expenses for the month, and you either have money left over or not each month.

If you are spending more than your income, look over the list of expenses and see where you can reduce them. Some of them may be obvious, some might not. You will need to prioritize your life and your expenses for yourself.

Without a car payment, for example, can you get to work? If so, you might want to cut that. You can sell the car, for example, and eliminate the payment. Or, you can turn the car back to the dealer and have the debt go delinquent. Remember if you don't have a car, you don't have a car payment, auto insurance, and gasoline or fuel expenses. You might have public transport expenses, if you use that as a substitution. In that case be sure to update your budget to include whatever expenses you have to get to work each day.

If you trim your expenses and have enough money each month you'll be able to pay your debts. In that case, start paying your bills and get out of debt. You'll have to tighten up and not buy things you don't have money to buy.

This may sound hard, and it is.

Increase your income, and pay the debts

Another option is to look over your income sources and find an additional source of income. For example, a second job could give you enough income to offset the expenses and allow you to pay the debts in full. Again, this won't be an easy choice, but none of the choices you have at this point will be easy. You need to decide what will be right for your situation, and do it.

If you have more money each month than expenses, but you're just barely making ends meet, look over your expenses and cut where you can. Increase your income where you can. Pay off your debts.

How to pay off your debts faster

There's a bit of a "trick" to paying off your debts. You can take the slow road (which might take many, many years) of paying just the minimum payments on all debts you owe. Or, you can "trick the system" and pay them off much faster using a couple of secret tips. Here's how it works:

On your list of debts, write down next to each debt the monthly payment, and also the interest rate for that debt. Use the current interest rate, from the latest statement. If you don't know what it is or cannot find your statement, call the company and ask them what the interest rate is for that debt. THIS IS IMPORTANT so be sure to make note of each one.

Look at your budget.

Notice how much extra you have each month to spend to pay down your debts. If it's not a lot of money, that's all right, this will still work. If you can eliminate some optional expenses for a few months to work on this plan, do that and use the money for this right now.

Take the highest interest rate debt – let's say it's a credit card charging 34% interest. Pay the minimum payment PLUS the extra money you found in your budget this month, and make that extra payment on that debt.

For all the other debts, make only the minimum payments this month.

Keep working on eliminating optional or unnecessary items in your budget, and take the extra money you're saving and add it to the minimum payment on that highest interest rate debt next month.

Do this every month until that debt is paid in full.

(Now the REAL fun begins!)

Find the next-highest interest rate debt. Let's say it's a 24% interest rate credit card.

For all your other debts except this one, make only the minimum payments. But for this highest interest rate debt, make the minimum payment PLUS what you were paying on that paid-off 34% interest debt.

Continue paying extra on this debt each month until it's paid off.

Now look at your debts, and choose the highest interest rate debt, and use this same method to pay it off faster. By now you'll have what you used to pay toward two other debts, so this debt will go bye-bye a lot faster.

Use this method to eliminate all your debts faster and with less interest payments than other methods of payoff.

If none of these seem to be right for you, keep reading for more options.

Get a loan to pay your debts

If you have the credit available, you could "consolidate" your debts into one loan and pay off all the other debts with that one loan. This might be useful if your interest rates are too high and you can get a loan for a lower interest rate that can be paid off.

The advantage to this method is having just one loan payment each month. Another good point is you can get a fixed loan length and have the debt paid off in a definite time, rather than having a variable interest rate that goes on seemingly forever.

A credit card with 24% interest rate, balance of $10,000, making only minimum payments, will take about 29 years, 5 months to pay off, and total payments of $29,332 – nearly three times the amount borrowed.

The same $10,000 balance at 10% interest – but only making minimum payments – will take over 14 years to pay off!

If that $10,000 was being charged 34% interest, it will take more than 158 years to pay off using only minimum payments, and cost $50,494 – more than five times the amount borrowed. Excuse me – 158 YEARS??? Yes, that is not a typo. More than 1900 months of payments will be needed to pay off that debt. This is ridiculous, and another reason to avoid paying only minimum payments on a credit card debt.

$10,000 borrowed
10%, 24% and 34% interest rates

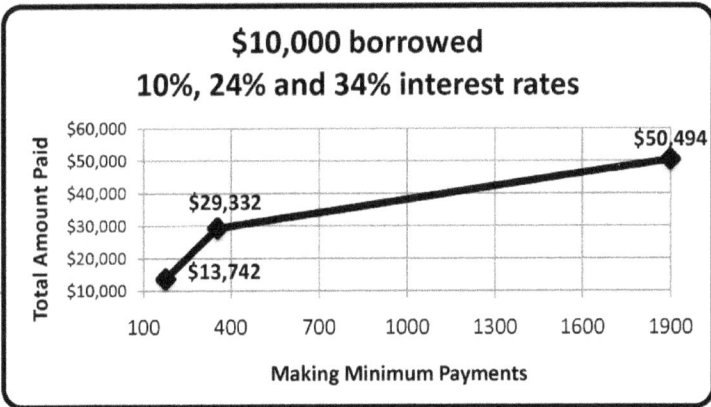

A major disadvantage to a consolidation loan is you have one large loan and still have credit cards that can be used. If you don't revise your spending habits you could end up in more debt very quickly.

BEWARE if you think borrowing against your home is the answer. You would be trading "unsecured" debts for "secured" debts. If you don't make the payments, your house could be sold to pay the debt, and you would be out of your home.

Take this step carefully, if you decide you should, and keep close watch on your spending. If this works for you then you WILL be out of debt someday when the consolidation loan is paid.

Contact your creditors and get them to extend the loan, or lower the interest rate, or work out a payment plan so you can pay off the debts

If your debt is a loan payment, you can contact the lender and ask for an extended time to pay back the loan. This means your monthly payment will be lowered (you will probably pay more interest in the long run, but if you need the monthly payment lowered this is an option for you).

If you are not behind in your payments, but you foresee this will happen soon, you can contact each of your creditors and ask them to lower the interest rate. The reason you would want this is so you can pay the debt off sooner.

This is important enough to repeat: if you are paying $300 per month to a $10,000 credit card balance with a 34% interest rate, you'll pay more than $50,000 and take more than 158 years to pay off the card using only the minimum payment each month.

With that same $10,000 owed, at 24% interest, making minimum payments will take over 29 years and cost more than $29,000.

As a comparison – and to demonstrate the difference in "minimum payments" versus "fixed payments" consider this – at 24% interest you can pay off that card much faster with $300 every month (about 4 years 6 months if you make every payment $300). If you need to, you can lower your payment to, say, $250, and still pay off the card faster with the lower interest rate.

This graph demonstrates the difference it makes to pay off a $10,000 balance with a fixed monthly payment of $300, comparing interest rates of 10%, 24%, and 34%. You see the difference it makes: even at 34% interest you'd be paid off in about 9 years, compared with "forever" if you made only the minimum payment each month.

$10,000 borrowed
10%, 24% and 34% interest rates

Total Amount Paid

$35,000
$30,000
$25,000
$20,000
$15,000
$10,000
$5,000

$11,764

$16,644

$31,035

40

56

104

Making $300 Monthly Payment

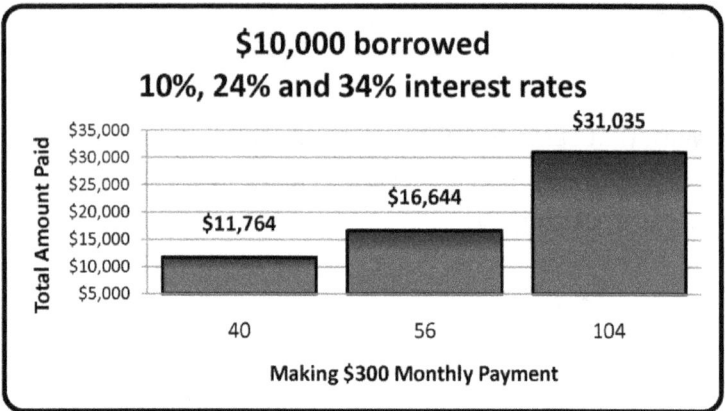

If you're worried about what to say or how to say it, go the The Motley Fool website **www.fool.com** and read their script for dealing with this exact topic. Search for "Get It Done: Negotiate With Your Lender" on their website and you'll find word-for-word what to say to get your better interest rate.

Another option is for "lump sum" payments that are due – in other words, large payments that are coming up soon. These are also called "balloon" payments. Contact the creditor and see if you can pay off the debt in monthly payments, and see how much time you can take to pay the loan. If you're having trouble making ends meet this could be what you need to make it through the next couple of years.

Option Two: Debt Management Plan (Credit Counseling)

Some creditors will offer a way for you to get the debt paid off within five years by lowering your interest rate and fixing your monthly payment. These plans are known as "debt management" plans. There are companies that offer to do this for you, however you can do this yourself. Companies that offer this service also call this service "credit counseling" because there is detailed budgeting done as part of this program. However, you've already done your detailed budget!

To get a debt management plan going, contact your creditors and explain what's going on with your finances and your bills. Ask them to put you on a debt management plan.

If you are using the forms on my website, **www.HowToSettleDebtsYourself.com**, you can record your hardship details and print a letter to send your creditors right from the site. Download the ***Hardship Letter*** form to your computer, type out your information, save it to your computer, print it, and mail or fax it to each creditor. You can also update your hardship as time goes on, and send revised letters any time you need.

"Hardship" is what the creditors listen to when you are explaining why you can't pay your debts, or need a modification in the terms of repayment, or why you're considering filing bankruptcy. "Hardship" can be: loss of job or income; divorce or spousal desertion; family illness; hospitalization; cutback of working hours; late on one payment and all the interest rates were suddenly pushed up to 39% and can no longer make even minimum payments on all cards; and other reasons why you cannot pay per their terms.

"Hardship" would not include reasons like: don't want to pay; took a cash advance on the card and didn't make any payments after that; moved to another state to avoid creditors; those would be examples of possible fraud, and could land you in jail.

Typically debt management plans result in your credit account being closed, so don't be surprised when that happens. Happily, you'll also get a fixed interest rate on the account, and the debt will be paid off in about five years if you make all the payments on time.

Alternatively, you could contact a credit counseling company to handle this procedure for you. Be aware this will require some fees. Frankly, you can do it yourself and save some money.

As an example, if the credit counseling company charges you $30 per month, and you're on their program five years, you'll pay $1,800 in fees to that company for doing something you can do yourself.

Also, you should be aware that the credit counseling companies often get paid by the credit card companies – so who are they really working for? You? Or the credit card companies? Who has more money to pay them? If you follow the money trail, you'll see debt management or credit counseling companies are more likely to follow the credit card companies' wishes than yours.

I recommend you arrange your own debt management plan and save that money to pay off your debts!

Option Three: Debt Settlement

Since this is the topic of Chapter Four, here is a summary:

With debt settlement (also called "debt negotiation"), you set aside some money each month (as much as you can) so you have money saved up to use for negotiation. You contact each of your creditors and offer a "lump sum" payment in exchange for full settlement on the debt. With this method you could pay 10% or 20% of the debt amount and be done, with nothing else due on that debt. There are some important points you'll want to be aware of so read Chapter Four thoroughly if you are going to use this method of taking care of your debts.

Option Four: Bankruptcy

Bankruptcy is for people who cannot pay their debts even at a lower amount. Typically a lawyer will handle this, representing you in court and filing the required paperwork. You may need to appear in court and give your side of the story, explaining to the judge why you need to file bankruptcy.

Your court case will become a public record. The bankruptcy judgment will stay on your credit report for a number of years (usually 7 or 10). If you are asked "Have you ever filed bankruptcy?" on a credit or employment application you will need to answer "yes" if you have ever filed for bankruptcy.

There are several kinds of bankruptcy; here is a brief summary of the types you may need:

Bankruptcy Chapter 7 (eliminates all debts except some secured debts, varies by state)

From Wikipedia: "Generally, a trustee will sell most of the debtor's assets to pay off creditors. However, certain assets of the debtor are protected to some extent. For example, Social Security payments, unemployment compensation, and limited values of your equity in a home, car, or truck, household goods and appliances, trade tools, and books are protected. However, these exemptions vary from state to state."[5]

You should consult a lawyer if you want to file Chapter 7 bankruptcy. Laws vary by state, with some allowing you to keep your home depending on the equity involved. Essentially with Chapter 7 bankruptcy, your non-exempt assets are sold to satisfy your debts by court order. (There are many other requirements so please research this more fully and contact a lawyer if you choose this route.) If you do not qualify for this type of bankruptcy you may need to file a Chapter 13 instead.

Bankruptcy Chapter 11 (mostly for businesses)

From Wikipedia: "In Chapter 11, the debtor retains ownership and control of its assets and is re-termed a debtor in possession ("DIP"). The debtor in possession runs the day to day operations of the business while

---

[5] Source: *7/20/2011* **http://en.wikipedia.org/wiki/Bankruptcy**

creditors and the debtor work with the Bankruptcy Court in order to negotiate and complete a plan."[6]

This type of bankruptcy is a restructuring of your debts so you can remain in business, while paying your creditors back what you owe them.

Bankruptcy Chapter 13 (repayment plan mandated by courts)

From Wikipedia: "In Chapter 13, the debtor retains ownership and possession of all of his or her assets, but must devote some portion of his or her future income to repaying creditors, generally over a period of three to five years. The amount of payment and the period of the repayment plan depend upon a variety of factors, including the value of the debtor's property and the amount of a debtor's income and expenses. Secured creditors may be entitled to greater payment than unsecured creditors."[7]

Similar to Chapter 11 but for individuals, this plan restructures your debts – mandated by the courts – and has you pay them back within three to five years.

---

[6] Source: *7/20/2011* **http://en.wikipedia.org/wiki/Bankruptcy**
[7] Source: *7/20/2011* **http://en.wikipedia.org/wiki/Bankruptcy**

The general rule is that if you do not qualify for a Chapter 7 bankruptcy plan, you will be moved into a Chapter 13 by decision of the bankruptcy judge if you qualify for a bankruptcy plan.

Option Five: Walk away from the debt

There are times when you just need to not pay the debt at all. In that case, you need to know about the Statute of Limitations in the state where you live.

The Statute of Limitations varies per state. It says that if there has been no activity on a debt for a certain number of years (this varies from state to state) the debt can no longer be collected by the creditor. Of course you still owe it, but the creditor cannot continue trying to collect on it. Many states have a limit of three years; a few are eight years or longer.[8]

There are moral repercussions to consider if you choose this. You have to decide if it's the right thing to do in your case. Obviously, if it's not your debt in the first place, you don't need to pay it and can walk away without guilt. If you owe a debt and refuse to pay it, for whatever reason, you should be sure you're doing the right thing for all parties to the transaction.

---

[8] Credit cards are considered "open" accounts in most states, and the Statute of Limitations can be different than, for example, a car loan or "promissory" account.

One more thing: you could be served with a lawsuit if you don't pay your debts. However, this could happen at any time for any reason. Even if the statute of limitations has run out, you could be sued for the debt by the lender or a collection agency. The Federal Trade Commission (FTC) has an article on their website called "Time-Barred Debts" that explains this very well and tells you what you can do if you are sued over a time-barred debt.

Here is an excerpt from that FTC alert:

"Most courts that have addressed the issue have ruled that the FDCPA [9] does not prohibit debt collectors from trying to collect time-barred debts, as long as they do not sue or threaten to sue you for the debt. If a debt collector sues you to collect a time-barred debt, you can have the suit dismissed by letting the judge know the debt is, indeed, time-barred." [10]

Notice that last sentence: *if you are sued for a debt that has gone beyond the Statute of Limitations, the*

---

[9] FDCPA stands for Fair Debt Collections Practices Act and is the law protecting consumers from illegal collection tactics.

[10] Source: *October 2004*

www.ftc.gov/bcp/edu/pubs/consumer/alerts/alt144.shtm

case can be dismissed in court. Read the full FTC alert to get all the information about this. Consult a lawyer if you would like legal advice.

You'll need to balance the pros and cons of this choice before you walk away from your debts. Also, be aware if you make ANY payment (even a few years later) on the debt, or acknowledge you owe that debt, it can start the statute of limitations clock all over again.

Statute of Limitations by State [11] [12] [13]

State	Promissory Note	Open Account
Alabama	6	3
Alaska	6	6
Arizona	5	3

---

[11] Source: *March 2011* **bankrate.com** and **nolo.com**.

[12] "Promissory Note" is normally a fixed contract, such as a mortgage or car loan, where there is an exact amount of time for the debt to be repaid.

[13] "Open Account" is for an open-ended contract, and credit cards normally fall in this category.

State	Promissory Note	Open Account
Arkansas	5	3
California	4	4
Colorado	6	6
Connecticut	6	6
Delaware	6	3
Florida	5	4
Georgia	6	4
Hawaii	6	6
Idaho	10	4
Illinois	6	5
Indiana	10	6
Iowa	5	5

State	Promissory Note	Open Account
Kansas	5	3
Kentucky	15	5
Louisiana	10	3
Maine	6	6
Maryland	6	3
Massachusetts	6	6
Michigan	6	6
Minnesota	6	6
Mississippi	3	3
Missouri	10	5
Montana	8	5
Nebraska	6	4

State	Promissory Note	Open Account
Nevada	3	4
New Hampshire	6	3
New Jersey	6	6
New Mexico	6	4
New York	6	6
North Carolina	5	3
North Dakota	6	6
Ohio	15	6
Oklahoma	5	3
Oregon	6	6
Pennsylvania	4	6
Rhode Island	10	10

State	Promissory Note	Open Account
South Carolina	3	3
South Dakota	6	6
Tennessee	6	6
Texas	4	4
Utah	6	4
Vermont	6	6
Virginia	6	3
Washington	6	3
West Virginia	6	5
Wisconsin	10	6
Wyoming	10	8

Verification of Debt

If you're not sure the debt is yours, use the ***Debt Verification Letter*** to have the creditor prove you owe the debt. [14]

Some people use the Verification of Debt procedure as a "stall tactic" to postpone collection activity for 30 days, knowing they owe the debt but trying to stall collection. This can backfire. Some creditors will automatically sue a client who is using this stall tactic. Use with caution.

But if you don't think the debt is yours, get the creditor to verify you owe the amounts claimed. If they cannot prove it, they cannot continue to collect.

---

[14] Letters mentioned in this book are available in the Appendix, and also on my website **www.HowToSettleDebtsYourself.com** – see Appendix for the username and password you'll need.

DATE

CREDITOR NAME
CREDITOR ADDRESS
CREDITOR CITY, STATE, ZIP

RE: YOUR ACCOUNT NUMBER

Dear Sirs,

I received your request for payment on this alleged debt but I don't agree that I owe this debt.

Please provide verification of debt.

Mail your documentation to:

YOUR MAILING ADDRESS
CITY, STATE, ZIP

In the meantime, please do not continue to collect this disputed debt until proper verification is provided.

Sincerely,

YOUR NAME
YOUR ADDRESS
YOUR CITY, STATE, ZIP

Chapter Three – Your Decision

This is where you need to study the information you've gathered about your debts, your income, and your expenses. After reviewing all that, and figuring out ways to cut expenses and increase income, the question becomes, "What do I do with my debts and bills?"

If you haven't already found the perfect solution, you may need some "real life" scenarios to help you. A few examples might help you decide.

Scenario: Single, young, with student loans and credit card debts

Problem: Suppose you are a single person out of college with $25,000 in student loans and another $15,000 in credit card debts. You don't have much difficulty paying your monthly bills but you feel hemmed in because you can't have the "good life" you were expecting when you graduated.

Solution: Make a budget and stick to it. Stop using credit cards for a while. Pay off your debts faster by paying more on them each month until they are gone. If you pay extra on the highest interest rate card or loan each month (and minimums on the rest) you will be out of debt fastest.

Scenario: Middle-aged, divorced, credit card debts with high interest rates

Problem: Let's say you are a middle-aged recently-divorced person with $30,000 in credit card debts and a low-paying job. You're barely making ends meet from paycheck to paycheck and are seriously considering bankruptcy. The divorce was costly and the income is not enough for one person to keep everything afloat without a lot of juggling. Your interest rates are fairly high because you missed a payment about six months ago, although you've diligently paid on time since then.

Solution One: Contact your creditors and ask for an interest rate reduction. If the first call doesn't work, wait a few days and call again (you'll get another customer service person who may be more helpful). Ask to speak to a supervisor if you feel you are being unfairly treated, and you may get what you want.

Solution Two: Contact your creditors and get on a debt management plan, where you'll pay off all your debts in five years or less, with a fixed interest rate. Be ready to go "cash only" when you do this because your credit cards will most likely be frozen until they are paid in full.

Scenario: Over your head in debts and cannot meet minimum payments

Problem: You're over your head in debt and cannot make your minimum payments. In fact, you've stopped paying your credit cards completely, and now they are calling to remind you about the missed payments. You know you should pay them but don't have any solutions.

Solution: Review your budget and cut out every expense you can. Set aside SOME money each month to start saving up to settle your debts. Contact your creditors either by phone or mail and let them know you want to pay but have some financial hardships preventing you from paying. Tell them you will contact them as soon as you have some money for them. Read Chapter Four for more specific details on how to conduct this conversation to your advantage. When you're ready, negotiate a settlement on each account until all are settled. Be prepared to go "cash only" and take a credit score hit while you are in this program, but you may be able to get out of it within a few years or less.

Scenario: Owe more than you own and can never pay it all back

Problem: You owe more than you can ever pay back, even if you pay the rest of your life. You don't have any equity in your home, you own an older car, and have no valuable assets to speak of. You want to pay your debts but just can't.

Solution One: Consider debt negotiation. If you're not able to pay your monthly payments you might be able to set aside whatever money you CAN afford into a savings account and use that to negotiate a settlement with your creditors. See Chapter Four for the procedure to follow.

Solution Two: Contact an experienced bankruptcy attorney about Chapter 7 bankruptcy. If you qualify, your debts will be discharged and you can start a fresh life. You will have the bankruptcy notation on your credit report for seven years and may have a hard time establishing credit for a while, so be prepared to pay cash for whatever you buy. However, you will be able to start over and not have the debts weighing you down.

Scenario: Not sure if you should choose Debt Management or Debt Settlement

Problem: You've done your budget and things look pretty grim. There's just not enough money to go around each month. You think you might like to try debt settlement, but you think debt management might be the better road to travel. You wonder if you could do both?

Solution: Yes, you can. Start with a debt management plan and if for some reason you cannot keep up the payments then switch to a debt settlement plan. And if for some reason that can't work for you (perhaps additional hardship occurs) then go to bankruptcy as a last resort. You'll be able to document your path to resolving money troubles and probably provide a good case for bankruptcy by that point.

With these examples, where do you fit? Figure out your best solution and get started now!

Chapter Four - Settle it yourself

From now on, the assumption is that you've decided to settle your debts. Even if you're still not sure, and think you might need to file bankruptcy, you may want to go through the debt settlement process first, and if that's successful then you can avoid some of the downsides of bankruptcy.

Let's get started!

First Step: Contact Your Creditors

Your creditors may not know you are having financial difficulties. You may be paying on time. They don't know you're going to stop paying or are about to start missing payments. The first thing you will do in a debt negotiation process is contact each of them and let them know what's going on with the payments.

It could be you've already started missing payments, or even stopped paying altogether. In that case you're probably getting phone calls politely reminding you that a payment hasn't been received. If it's been a few months since the last payment, those phone calls could be 5 - 10 times a day (or more) and automated – on an automatic computer dialer – and they can get quite annoying. The phone rings all day long and you might not want to answer just to talk to someone about your inability to pay.

The guilt feelings you may be experiencing can be painful and deter you from wanting to talk to the creditors even more than before. Some creditors or collectors are effective at making people feel so bad about not being able to pay that they make a payment just to make the collector "go away." This isn't going to solve the problem in the long run but it may buy you some temporary relief from that collector. If you have more than one debt, there will be collectors for each of them calling. Most creditors can see activity on all your accounts using your credit report, so word will get around that you paid one and not the others. Then you'll get calls (and letters) demanding you pay each of them. This makes a busy life and you feel like you are defending yourself all the time.

By contacting your creditors you start taking control of the situation, at least a little bit, and stop being defensive. Ideally, you contact them before they try to contact you. But if they've already started, then contacting them will give them at least some hope that they'll get paid someday. After all, they did loan the money, and they would like to get paid. Looking at it from their viewpoint, they want to get paid. Looking at it from your viewpoint, you want to pay them but you can't afford to pay them all of what is owed right now. So, contact them and tell them you want to pay them but can't right now, but you're working on it.

On my website **www.HowToSettleDebtsYourself.com** are sample letters you can send your creditors to let them know what is going on and that you will keep them posted on your progress. Download the letters to your computer. Fill in your basic contact information. Then print, sign, and mail to your creditors at the mailing location listed on your monthly statement.

The ***Hardship Letter*** will give your creditors some hardship information and ask for more time to pay.

The main thing to start with – when you first contact your creditors – is to tell them you are having financial problems and give them some of your hardship information. You do NOT have to tell them how much you make, where you work, what your mother's phone number is, or anything like that. You might get asked all of those questions and more; after all, they want to know how to collect the money and want to know every avenue they can pursue to get paid. You will want to tell them some version of why you can't pay right now.

You do not have to call your creditors; you can write them a letter with this information. Sometimes, especially if the phone calls are rough for you or if you get flustered talking on the phone with the creditor, it is best to send a letter. You can also fax the information to them in a letter. Sometimes it works best to start with a letter, follow up with a fax, and after a few weeks or months then make the phone calls. It's not always the case but this is an option if it helps you get it done.

When you call (or send the letter) be sure to explain your hardship in as much detail as you can. Try to put yourself in the shoes of the person or company you owe: If you were owed money, what would make you understand that the debtor can't pay you right now, but you might be able to get paid later? That's the kind of letter (or phone call) you need to make. That is why the "hardship" information is so important. It tells the creditor you have a legitimate reason for non-payment right now, and lets them know you are not just shrugging off the obligation and that you really do need some help from them.

Besides mailing a letter, you can also use the **Hardship Letter** and read from it while you are talking with your creditors. It can help keep you on track during the conversation if you tend to get flustered talking with them.

TODAY'S DATE

CREDITOR NAME
CREDITOR MAILING ADDRESS
CREDITOR CITY, STATE, ZIP

RE: YOUR ACCOUNT NUMBER

Dear Sirs,

I'm writing to let you know I'm having trouble paying my debts. I am working to resolve this but wanted you to understand my current situation. The reason I'm unable to pay right now is:

ENTER YOUR HARDSHIP INFORMATION. EXAMPLES OF HARDSHIP ARE:
  LOSS OF JOB
  WORK HOURS CUT BACK
  HOSPITAL STAY (SELF)
  HOSPITAL STAY (FAMILY)
  CARING FOR FAMILY MEMBER
  SEPARATION OR DIVORCE
  DEATH IN FAMILY
  BUSINESS FAILURE
  SEVERE ILLNESS OR INJURY WITH INABILITY TO WORK
  WHATEVER IS YOUR SITUATION – MAKE YOUR OWN STATEMENT
  OF FACTS

I appreciate your understanding while I'm recovering from this difficult time. I hope to be able to contact you soon with more information.

Sincerely,

YOUR NAME
YOUR ADDRESS
YOUR CITY, STATE ZIP

A Sample Conversation with Your Creditor

Here is a sample conversation you might have with a creditor when you first call:

Creditor: Customer Service, may I help you?

You: Yes, I'm calling because I won't be able to make my next payment.

Creditor: I'm sorry to hear that, let's verify your account number so I can access your account.

(Go through the account verification process.)

Creditor: Thanks for waiting; I have your account records now. Tell me, what is the problem?

You: I'm not going to be able to make my next payment. I've [lost my job; had my hours cut back; gotten a divorce; been in the hospital; been taking care of an ill family member; whatever is a brief version of your hardship]. I'm working to catch up and I think it will be a few months before I can pay something.

Creditor: All right, I understand. I can place your account on hold for a month. Do you think you'll be able to make a payment next month?

You: No, I don't think I will. I would like you to notate my account to show I called. May I get your name and phone extension, so I can make a note for my records?

Creditor: (should give you the name or "agent number" – be sure to write this down.) Will you be able to get money from some other source to pay your next payment?

You: Thanks, I will check on that and get back to you. Thank you for helping me.

Creditor: (may try to make more conversation, to get more information from you.)

You: I'm sorry, I can't talk more right now, I have many other calls to make, thank you again for your help. I need to go now. Good bye. (Hang up without engaging in more information, but stay polite as you can.)

Make a note of this call, including the contact person you spoke to. Follow up with a letter to the company and include your hardship info and that you will contact them again soon. On my website download the

Creditor Contact Letter and use it to send the creditor a written summary of your conversation.

File the records in your file folder. Remember, it's easier to keep focused if you have a file for your creditors and can review it when you are ready to negotiate.

When speaking with your creditors to explain your hardship, be polite but firm about why you cannot pay in full right now. Stay focused.

Some buzzwords you'll want to remember

You'll find some words being said pretty fast when you're talking with creditors. Some of these will be used in letters to you. Here is a summary of some of the most commonly misunderstood terms used by creditors so you know what they're talking about.

Hardship

This is the reason you're not able to pay your debts on time, or the reason you have stopped paying your creditors, or the reason you think you're about to be unable to pay on time. A hardship is NOT "I just don't feel like paying" – that would be potentially FRAUD which could get you a prison term if prosecuted and proven. A real hardship may have been in the works for a long time (borrowing to pay routine living expenses) or may have been a sudden occurrence (catastrophic life event such as divorce or hospitalization or job loss). A hardship is what is preventing you from being on your feet and able to pay your bills on time.

Bankruptcy

Covered in Chapter Two, bankruptcy is a court-ordered action that either eliminates all debts, or forces a partial payment based on your income. It is useful for getting a new start without burdensome debts if you qualify and need this option.

Some people may advise you to threaten bankruptcy so your creditors want to settle with you. That might work but it could also backfire on you if you are really not qualified for bankruptcy. A creditor could "call your bluff" and make you feel tongue-tied and on the defensive.

If bankruptcy really is an option you might have to consider, then it's okay to say it, but not as an idle threat. You want to be as truthful as you can. As Mark Twain wrote, "If you tell the truth you don't have to remember anything." The creditors keep notes of conversations with their clients. If you change your story from one phone call to the next, they'll know it and you'll be mistrusted.

Insolvency

When you settle a debt, you've "earned" that amount in income, at least according to the Internal Revenue Service (IRS), and you are required to report that "earned income" on your tax return for that year.

"INSOLVENCY" is when your income and assets are inadequate to cover your expenses and liabilities. If you can document insolvency the IRS allows a tax break on the forgiven debt amount. Use Form 982 (available on the IRS website) to show insolvency; file that form with your tax return. [15]

Charge off

When a creditor determines a debt is "uncollectable" or "unlikely to be collected" they can get a tax write-off for the full amount of the debt owed. When their accountants "write off" that bad debt, they call it a "charge off" – all this means is that the creditor is going to get a tax deduction for that debt amount.

---

[15] See end of Chapter Four, "Will I owe taxes on the settlement?" for more information on how to file Form 982 when needed.

A charge off can mean you are able to get a better settlement, because often those debts are then "sold" to a collection agency for pennies on the dollar. Collection agencies are then willing to settle for, say, dimes on the dollar and they still make a good profit.

Sometimes a charge off means the creditor is simply transferring the debt to another division of their company that deals with harder-to-collect debt amounts. In that case, the charged-off debt is still owned by the original creditor. They may still be willing to settle for a lower amount because anything they receive will be income – and more than they would have received if the debt wasn't paid at all.

Creditors can "charge off" debts and then pursue legal actions (they could sue you to collect the debt in court). When you are speaking with your creditors you may have one tell you, "This account is about to be CHARGED OFF" – as if that was a threat or as if that means you'll be in big trouble. It is okay to ask, "What does that mean? What will be your next action? What is your company policy for charged-off debts?" You may as well find out what they mean when these terms are being thrown around. Ask! You have the right to know what they are talking about.

Simply put, "charge off" is an accounting term that means the debt has become a tax deduction for the creditor, and further collection activity may be tried next.

Statute of Limitations

As mentioned in Chapter Two, there is a statute of limitations for debts. If your debts are older than that limit then creditors are not longer allowed to collect on them. (You still owe the debt, but they can't collect.)

Some states have statutes as short as two or three years. Some are as long as 10 years. You will need to check with your state's laws to discover the statute of limitations for your state. [16]

Just because your debts may be older than the statute of limitations doesn't mean you don't owe the debt. Until the debt is paid, settled, or otherwise resolved IN WRITING from your creditor, it's really still your debt. The statute of limitations only says they can't collect on the debt any longer. It doesn't say you don't still owe the debt.

---

[16] See the Appendix for a table of all states' Statute of Limitations.

Morally or ethically you may want to make sure your debts are paid or settled or otherwise fully resolved. That way, you don't have to worry about them, and you don't fear any consequences from non-payment.

(Some employers will run credit checks as a routine policy before offering employment or promotion. If your debts are paid or settled or resolved, you are in a stronger position than if they are still outstanding.)

Original creditor

An ORIGINAL CREDITOR is the firm you borrowed from in the first place, or the company that gave you credit to begin with.

Examples:

For the **Southwest Visa** card, the original creditor is **Chase Bank**;

For the **Banana Republic Visa** card, the original creditor is **GE Money Bank**;

If an account is at a collection agency, the original creditor could be (for example):

Hampton Hospital – being collected by **General Services, PLC**

or

Joe's Mufflers and Tires – being collected by **Uncle Vinnie's Collection Agency**

Collection agency

When an original creditor charges off an account and turns it over to another (third party) company to collect the debt, that third party is now acting as a debt collector. Those companies are loosely called COLLECTION AGENCIES. They could be a mom-and-pop company, or a large nationwide company, or even a law firm that specializes in collecting debts. All of them are essentially debt collectors.

Each of these companies needs to follow some consumer-protective laws and you can arm yourself with better information about those laws. You should review the section about the FAIR DEBT COLLECTION PRACTICES ACT to get more information about your rights. It will save you time, hassles, and may help you get an even better settlement with any creditor who has violated any portion of the FDCPA.

Seriously, learn this and use it to your advantage!

FCRA

The FAIR CREDIT REPORTING ACT is designed to protect you from erroneous credit information that may sneak into your credit report. Originally begun in 1970, it was revised in 2003 to give you better access to what information is being collected about you, and to better protect your identity. Even so, you should be aware of the act and its parts so you can use it to protect yourself and your credit report.

There are three major credit reporting agencies:

Experian

TransUnion

Expedia

Each of these agencies may receive information from your creditors; some creditors report to all three, others only to one or two. You should review the information on your credit report at least once annually. In fact, the federal government has an online credit reporting retrieval site that allows you to get a copy of your credit report once a year AT NO CHARGE.

Go to **www.annualcreditreport.com** to get a copy of your credit report. You can also call a toll-free number listed on that website to get your free credit report.

Why would you want to see your credit report? For one thing, probably 30-40% of individuals have errors on their credit report. It's estimated 25% (one in four) have errors serious enough to be denied credit. [17] Examples: not your debt; not your address; wrong phone numbers; wrong social security numbers; old debt from ex-spouse; debt from parents or children. You'll want to clean this stuff up! You don't want to pay debts that are not yours, and you don't want debts that you've paid to show up on your credit report.

FDCPA

The FAIR DEBT COLLECTIONS PRACTICES ACT was enacted in 1978 and regulates what collectors can or cannot do to collect a debt owed. Here are some key points you should be aware of so you are not taken

---

[17] Source: *October 2004* **bankrate.com**

advantage of when someone is contacting you to collect a debt:

- They cannot attempt to collect more than you owe. The amount being collected must be per the contract and not be inflated or have additional non-contractual amounts added.
- They cannot collect fees or added charges that are not in the contract you signed.
- They cannot call repeatedly or in a harassing manner, or before 8:00 a.m. or after 9:00 p.m., or during a time that would be harassment (for example, if you sleep days and work nights, they cannot call you during your sleeping time).
- They cannot use profane language or issue threats of violence to yourself or your property
- They cannot threaten a lawsuit, garnishment, repossession of property, or other action if they don't intend or cannot take that action.
- They cannot inform anyone else about your debt illegally – this means they can't call your parents or children and tell them you owe money, nor can they call your employer or a neighbor and say you owe a debt.
- They cannot contact others to find your location more than once – in other words, they can't call

your next-door neighbor to "find you" and then call again later to "find you" – only once can someone else be contacted to locate you unless false information was given the first time.

- They cannot call your place of employment if you tell them you cannot be contacted there.

- They must send you a written notice giving you the opportunity to dispute the debt, and they must send this within 5 days of trying to collect the debt. You then have 30 days to dispute the debt, and during that dispute process they must cease trying to collect the debt if you have disputed it, until they provide proof of the debt to you (in writing).

- They must cease attempts to contact you to collect the debt if you have informed them in writing they must cease collecting. At that point they cannot contact you again except by mail to tell you they have ceased collection efforts, or they will be definitely taking certain actions (such as a lawsuit). But otherwise they must stop collection actions.

This is not an all-inclusive list of FDCPA violations but gives you an overview. The full list can be found on the FTC's website at **www.ftc.gov** – search for "FDCPA" and there you can read the full text of the statute.

You should be aware of the various FDCPA violations and be alert for them, because you can use them if they occur to get a more favorable settlement. If the collector is violating the FDCPA you should document the violation, date, time, and names and phone numbers if at all possible. A letter to the collector documenting the violation with a copy sent to your state's Attorney General and also to the Federal Trade Commission may help you with your negotiation. Violations of the FDCPA carry a fine of up to $1,000 *per violation* and can be a useful negotiation tool for you to have when needed.

For example, if the collection agent called in a harassing manner, and you have documented it, this is what you can do:

- Write a letter to the company with copies of the letters you sent to the regulators (as above),
- Offer to settle the account for (some amount, perhaps 10% of the balance), and
- Offer to cease pursuing other FDCPA remedies if the account is settled satisfactorily.

Legal threats

Let's face it: lawsuits happen. But here's a little-known fact – sometimes you get a letter that LOOKS LIKE a lawsuit and it's not. You need to know the difference so you can respond properly.

Know the difference between a demand letter and a summons. A "demand letter" says something like, "You need to respond to this letter which is demanding you pay the amount you owe by law." A "summons" is also sometimes called a "Summons and Complaint" or sometimes called an "Order to Appear" which means you need to show up in court. Lawyers can send out "demand letters" and they can look very official but they don't mean you need to show up in court (not yet). You need to read the letter and see what it is saying and then you'll know what you're dealing with.

If you get a demand letter – or a summons – and you are not sure what to do then you may want to consult a lawyer. There are many lawyers who will give you 15 or 30 minutes of their time for free, as a consultation, and you may want to talk to one of them. You can also seek help from various prepaid legal services. Additionally, you can ask for a lawyer if you cannot afford one and you are being sued, these are called "Public Defenders" and can be very good at their profession; if you need one be sure to ask the court for your right to legal representation.

Procedures in your jurisdiction for service of process, and how to respond.

It is beyond the scope of this book to detail each section of the U.S. court system and their various procedures. Many courts are similar and general information is available on the internet or in your local public library.

Sometimes, you can be "served" a summons BY MAIL – and it's perfectly legal! Other locations require the sheriff to appear in person and give you the summons in person. It all depends on where you live and what the local rules are.

If you receive a summons, you can ignore it (not recommended); get some legal advice (probably a good idea); respond to it in court by yourself (okay but maybe not the best idea); have a lawyer help you respond in court (probably a better idea); and you can even try to work out a settlement before you get to court. *You can even settle the debt in court*. All of these options are available to you. And if you try one and it doesn't work you can try another option. Keep trying to settle your debt, don't give up, and don't let a lawsuit get you upset.

If you don't know what your options are for responding to a summons, contact your local courthouse and find out. Ask for help, and the clerk is supposed to help you. You do pay their salaries with your taxes and they are supposed to give you assistance. It may be easier to get help if you go in person, or it may be easier to get help if you call. You can always call and ask – "Which do you prefer? That I call or visit to get help on how to respond to this lawsuit?" The clerk will probably tell you what is easier for him or her, and that's how they'll be more willing to help you. You really don't have anything to lose by asking, so get the help you need.

Garnishment

To "garnish" means a court orders a third party (such as your employer) to hold back what is owed to you, and pay it to someone else. You are the "garnishee" and the other person who receives the money is the "garnisher" and the entire process is called "garnishment." Could be your wages, a tax refund, or some other income you think you'll be receiving that ends up garnished. In any case, the money doesn't go to you but to your creditor.

Not all states allow wage garnishment, and each state's rules are different. You can search online for the wage garnishment rules in your state. Or, call your local courthouse and find out.

Lien

A "lien" is someone's right to hold your property to satisfy a debt you owe. They don't take your property, but they have a claim against it so that when you sell, they have to be paid. A common example of a lien is a mortgage. When you sell your house, the mortgage gets paid off first, and you get anything left over.

Levy

A "levy" comes about after a court judgment. It is defined as "to seize or attach (property) in accordance with the judgment of a court" (Collins Dictionary). If you get fined for a traffic ticket, for example, the court will "levy a fine" which you will pay.

Stipulated Judgment

When you have a judgment against you, in other words when the creditor has won their case in court and you are now ordered to pay somehow, you can still work out a deal with the creditor. For example, "pay $100 per month until fully paid" and then the creditor won't try to garnish your wages or force you to sell your home or whatever other remedies they could use to collect. This deal you worked out is called a "stipulated judgment" because if you keep to your side of the deal, they have to keep to their side of the deal and leave things alone. The "stipulated" part means there are rules, and if those are followed, the judgment is put on hold while the rules are being followed.

Sometimes a stipulated judgment is your best bet when you need to protect your wages and you can be garnished.

Summary of initial contact

- Contact each creditor and explain your hardship.

- Ask for the collections specialist if you're not already transferred there.

- State your case, briefly, why you cannot pay now.

- Be polite but firm that you can't send money now.

- Be aware of the guilt they'll try to make you feel and don't give up. Remain firm to your plan.

- Ask for more time to pay; don't promise anything.

- Don't pay any money without a written settlement offer.

- Be polite, but don't waver from your position.

- If there are FDCPA violations, document them fully.

- Be sure to get the name and telephone number of the person you're speaking with.

- Hang up when YOU are done; control the call.

- Follow up with a letter documenting your initial conversation.

DATE

CREDITOR NAME
CREDITOR MAILING ADDRESS
CREDITOR CITY, STATE, ZIP

Regarding: Account # **YOUR ACCOUNT NUMBER**

Dear Sirs,

This letter is to confirm the telephone conversation I had today with your representative regarding my account.

As I explained, I am unable to continue making monthly payments on my account because **BRIEFLY LIST YOUR HARDSHIP**.

I want to satisfy this debt but am unable to do so at this time. I would appreciate any assistance you can offer.

I am working to resolve my situation as quickly as I can. I hope to have this resolved within **LIST YOUR EXPECTED TIMEFRAME**.

Thank you for your attention to this account.

Best regards,

YOUR NAME
YOUR ADDRESS
YOUR CITY, STATE, ZIP

Next Step: How to negotiate a settlement

You'll sometimes get a settlement offer right away when you call to give your hardship. Often this won't be the best offer you'll get (although the collector may SAY, "This is the best I can offer you.") Sometimes a better offer will be given by another collector at that office, sometimes the debt needs to be sent to a "third party collector" or a collection agency and then you'll get a better offer. If the debt is sold to a "debt buyer" they probably paid pennies on every dollar owed; in that case, if you settled for 10 percent of the total debt they'd still make a huge profit (and you would also benefit).

It is a good idea to find out who you're talking to: the original creditor (for example, the creditor is *Chase Bank* and you have a debt for a *Chase Visa*); an in-house collection agent (working directly for *Chase Bank* in one of their regional offices); a third-party collection agency (such as *Rapid Recovery*); an in-house law firm (such as *JPMorgan Chase Legal Department*); a third-party law firm (such as *Frederick J Hanna*); a small-town lawyer (*Michael Jones, Esq.*, in Kalamazoo); or a debt buyer (such as *Midland Funding*).

If you are talking to the original creditor or to their in-house counsel, you will want to make sure they understand your hardship thoroughly. They may have policies that prevent them from negotiating with you as favorably as you might like. However, these things can be negotiated. If you can get a supervisor or a person with a bit more "pull" in the organization you can explain what you can offer and appeal to their good nature to get your offer approved. You can always try this!

It may take one, five, or fifteen phone calls before you work out a settlement that you can accept. Be persistent. Keep notes of your conversations and store them in your file folder.

Perhaps the creditor is not offering any settlement to you. In that case you can make the first move. Say, "I would like to settle this account. Will you accept (name a dollar amount that you'd like to pay) as SETTLEMENT IN FULL?"

Use those words – **SETTLEMENT IN FULL** – to make sure they know what you want.

If the person you are talking to does not accept your offer, but you think it's a reasonable offer, you can ask to speak to a supervisor. You may have to persist or ask several times. That's okay.

Be polite and don't get upset over whatever the collector says to you. If you notice FDCPA violations (or you think they might be) then make a note of them so you can document the inappropriate statement in a follow-up letter. This might help you get a good settlement.

If you can get a settlement worked out in this first phone call, good job! Be sure to follow up with a letter documenting the conversation and agreement.

DO NOT SEND MONEY WITHOUT A WRITTEN SETTLEMENT OFFER FROM THE CREDITOR. In that offer, be sure it states the creditor will accept your payment as FULL SETTLEMENT for the total debt and that no more collection activity will occur once paid, and that the major credit bureaus will be notified the account is PAID.

Sometimes the account will be notated "SETTLED" or "PAID LESS THAN AGREED" or some other somewhat negative statement. As long as the balance is updated as ZERO and the account is PAID then you got what you need. Anything better than that is good for you.

Your credit score was already affected badly when your accounts went delinquent. When the debts start getting paid off, your credit score can start to recover. That can help you buy a home or car in the future, and may help for employment.

Settlements can be made in payments, for example over three months or even six months or more. Just remember you need to make ALL payments before the account is really settled. If you make some payments and not the rest, the settlement offer will be voided and you'll have to start all over.

You can offer a settlement in payments. Example, you owe $10,000, and are offering to settle for $2,000, paid in $500 payments for four months. After the fourth payment is made on time, the account will be fully settled. [18]

---

[18] On my website is the **Settlement Offer From You** letter.

TODAY'S DATE

CREDITOR NAME
CREDITOR MAILING ADDRESS
CREDITOR CITY, STATE, ZIP

Regarding: Account # **YOUR ACCOUNT NUMBER**

Dear Sirs,

This letter is to confirm the telephone conversation I had today with your representative regarding my account.

As I explained, I am unable to continue making monthly payments on my account because **BRIEFLY LIST YOUR HARDSHIP**.

As we discussed our options your representative offered to settle my account IN FULL upon my payment of **AMOUNT YOU DISCUSSED** by **DATE OF PAYMENT**. I am interested and would like to receive a written settlement offer, on company letterhead, verifying these terms.

In the letter please state the account will be marked "PAID IN FULL" and a zero balance will be reported to the three major credit bureaus, and also that you will cease further collection activity on this account when that settlement payment is made.

You may send the written settlement offer to my address below. Thank you for your attention to this account.

Best regards,

YOUR NAME
YOUR ADDRESS
YOUR CITY, STATE, ZIP

Always send a copy of the settlement letter with your payments. Keep the original copy for your records.

NEVER SEND MONEY WITHOUT A WRITTEN SETTLEMENT AGREEMENT.

One more word of advice:

Be sure the person or firm you are dealing with has the authority to negotiate with you. For example, if you are speaking with a paralegal at the Law Offices of Frederick J Hanna about a Bank of America loan then make sure Bank of America has transferred the debt to Hanna's office. You can verify this by calling Bank of America and asking to speak to the collections department. When you get them on the phone, ask them about your account. If they say, "That account has been transferred to the Law Offices of Frederick J Hanna" then you know you're all right. If Bank of America says they own the account, then you need to work with B of A and not work with the person at the law firm. The original creditor is the one who can tell you where the account is located now.

Settlement "nuts and bolts" – How to get it DONE

- Contact each creditor and see what they can offer for a "settlement in full."

- If this is a good offer for you, ask for a settlement offer in writing.

- NEVER SEND MONEY WITHOUT A WRITTEN SETTLEMENT AGREEMENT.

- Don't promise anything.

- Make sure the debt is owned by the company where you're sending the payments.

- Be sure to get the name and telephone number of the person you're speaking with.

- Follow up with a letter documenting your conversation.

- When you receive the written settlement offer, send the money as directed, and on time. Keep copies of the check and the settlement offer. Send a copy of the settlement letter with your check.

Start saving money to have available for settling accounts.

This is important, because you will need to have a lump sum of money to pay the settlement once you've worked it out. You should not save the money at a bank where you owe money. In other words, if you owe Chase Bank on a credit card, don't save your money at a Chase Bank! (The banks have a "right of offset" written into your credit agreement and it means they can "offset" what you owe them by exercising their "right" to your money in their bank. You could wake up one day and have no cash in that account and find out it went to pay down your debt to them.)

Banks are merging all the time, so you'll need to be alert to your bank's affiliations with other banks. For example, Chase and Washington Mutual merged a few years ago so they're not separate banks any longer. Another example, years ago Crocker National Bank was acquired by Wells Fargo, and more recently Wachovia Bank was also acquired by Wells Fargo. Those three banks are now owned by the same bank.

In 2010, 157 banks were taken over, merged, or closed. In 2009 it was 140 banks. (For comparison, in

2008 there were 25 bank failures.) Through June 2011 there were more than 45 failed banks according to the FDIC's website (Federal Deposit Insurance Corporation, which insures the money you've deposited at the bank). You can view the up-to-date listing on their website at **www.fdic.gov** – search for "bank failure" to find the latest information, including past years.

Where can you keep your money while you are saving?

The money needs to be readily available when you're ready to make settlement offers. So you could put it aside into a mutual fund, or a money market account, as long as you can get it out pretty quickly. A few days should be fast enough.

Set aside as much as you can afford, regularly, without fail. You don't want to shortcut this step! You MUST, MUST, MUST set money aside so you can have money to settle your debts. If you don't, you'll fail in this process. You will need to discipline yourself to say "no" to expenditures and "yes" to setting aside money to settle your debts.

Consider this the first step toward making a savings account, and when you're done settling your debts you can continue putting aside money for savings.

If you get a settlement offer that you like, be sure to get a written offer with a firm deadline that you can meet before you send ANY money anywhere.

Do not send money without a written offer. **NEVER SEND MONEY WITHOUT AN OFFER IN WRITING.** You don't want the money you pay to be put in the wrong place. When you send a payment you will include a copy of the written settlement letter to make sure it gets properly applied to your account and helps eliminate your debt fully.

Do send the money on time. Don't be late! If you miss a payment date you invalidate the entire settlement process you went through and you may lose that settlement! Don't be late.

If you "blow" a settlement offer (don't comply with the terms), all monies paid will be considered payments toward the full balance due and will be disregarded in any future conversations on the creditor's side of the negotiations.

If you cannot reach a good settlement with one creditor, try another. Be polite but firm and say you will call back when you have more money to settle, and then call another creditor.

It is okay to let one know you'll call another to see if they'll accept your settlement; this can create a competition between them to your benefit.

Continue until you are done settling all accounts

You will continue this process, contacting each of your creditors, saving money, getting settlement offers, and making settlements until you are done settling all your debts.

Depending on how much you owe, and how much you can set aside, you should plan on one or two years of hard work to get through this process. Sometimes you can get it done faster, especially if you can get 10% settlements and can get assistance from family or friends to get cash faster.

Finally: What is a good settlement offer?

Wow, that is a good question. I'm glad you asked!

In more than 12,000 settlements (that I've seen) the average is around 40% (this means pay $40 to settle $100 in debt). Some settlements are much lower, for example around 10%. Some settlements are higher, say about 70%. But most fall in the "definitely less than 50%" range, and most of those are less than 40% settlements.

If you can get a settlement offer that is less than 20% of what you owe, you've gotten a very good settlement offer.

Your settlement offers will depend on your hardship. If you have an extreme hardship you can get a better settlement offer. From the creditor's viewpoint, "any money is better than no money" and with a severe hardship they don't think they'll get much money, so they're willing to settle for much less.

A couple of years ago Bank of America was routinely offering 20% settlements. If the hardship was very good they would settle for as low as 10%. These internal policies change so just decide what you can afford and stick with that amount.

It's okay to tell one creditor that another creditor has offered you a better settlement, but you wouldn't want to be obnoxious about it. Be matter-of-fact about the amount you can afford and deal with the person you have on the phone.

Think about it: if you owe $10,000 to a bank, and they are willing to accept $5,000 as a full settlement, didn't you just come out $5,000 ahead? Food for thought.

Try to get settlements below 30% in all cases. Aim for 25% settlements. So, if you owe $1,000, you would settle for $250.

Remember to have the money saved so you can pay these settlements on time when you get them!

Settlement Percentages – the Good, the Bad, the Ugly

A good baseline for debt settlement is to aim for less than 50% in any settlement. Anything greater than 60% is bad, and greater than 80% is downright ugly.

Less than 40% is good, and the goal is to aim for about 20% - 25% in all cases. In some cases this won't be realistic but it's what you're going for.

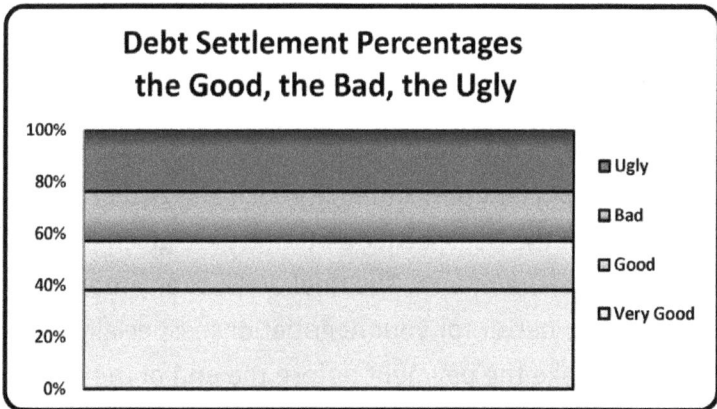

Debt Settlement Percentages the Good, the Bad, the Ugly

- Ugly
- Bad
- Good
- Very Good

When is a good time to settle debts?

Collectors have performance goals they want to meet, because it means bonus money for them. You can use this information to your advantage when you are trying to get a good settlement offer.

A minor performance goal is weekly, so Friday morning can bring some good offers. Collectors sometimes like to leave the office early on Friday, leaving subordinates in the office who might not give you the better deals. You can try to settle with them but if you don't feel you're getting a good enough settlement, politely say you'll think about it and hang up and call during another time to see if you can find a more receptive person for your discussion.

A more important performance goal is the end of the month, and the best settlement offers are given in the final days of the month. The final week of any month is going to be better for your negotiations, especially if you can make the payment before the end of the month. Your best offers will be between the 25th and 30th of each month – but remember, the payment will need to be received by the 30th. Don't get forced into a bad settlement and **NEVER SEND MONEY WITHOUT A WRITTEN SETTLEMENT AGREEMENT.**

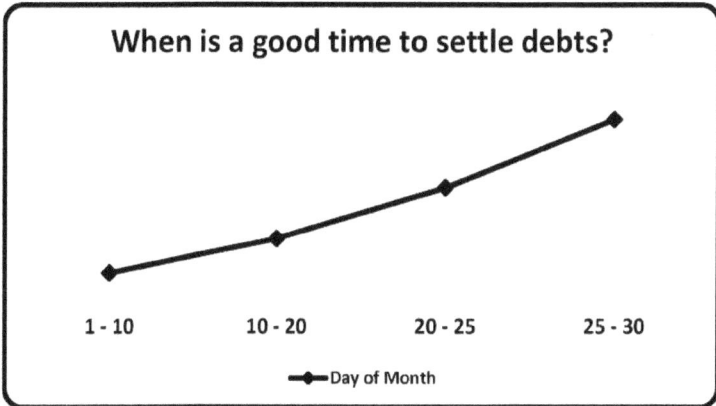

When is a good time to settle debts?

| 1 - 10 | 10 - 20 | 20 - 25 | 25 - 30 |

Day of Month

Each quarter (March, June, September, and December) will be another bonus period. Use this to your advantage!

The end of the year is probably the busiest and best (for you) settlement period, when companies are trying to clear bad debts off their books and get the maximum tax write-offs possible. However, creditors also want to have time off with their families during that time, so sometimes the best settlements are between the 15th and 23rd of December. Sometimes creditors will also be working those last few days of the year so you can try to settle then, too.

I hope this information helps you get better settlements!

Will I owe taxes on the settlement?

Yes, if you settle a debt for less than is owed, and the amount you don't have to pay is more than $600, you will owe taxes.

Here's how it works: The part of the debt you don't pay (when you settle) will be a tax write-off for the creditor. The IRS calls that part "forgiven debt" and will allow the tax write-off for the creditor. The creditor will take that amount of forgiven debt as a "bad debt" tax deduction. The IRS will be looking to you to pay taxes on the amount of forgiven debt. Remember, it's money you borrowed, and didn't pay back, so it's like money you were given by the creditor. That's why the IRS considers it income (even though you might not).

One possibility to eliminate the tax is to file Form 982 with the IRS. The form's full name is "Reduction of Tax Attributes Due to Discharge of Indebtedness (and Section 1082 Basis Adjustment)" and that offers you an opportunity to tell the IRS you should have the taxes reduced because you are insolvent (that means you owe more than you can pay). You can find the form on the IRS's website. A tax preparer can help you fill out the form if the instructions are not clear. This form is very useful, so don't neglect to check it out. It's likely that most people who need to settle their debts could qualify to have their taxes reduced or eliminated due to insolvency (meaning, even if they sold all their assets they couldn't pay all their debts).

The IRS allows you to define insolvency BEFORE the debts are forgiven (settled). In other words, you take a look at what your financial situation was when you owed all the money, not after all the debts are settled. Using this definition most people who need debt settlement would be able to claim insolvency. To be certain, please consult a tax accountant if you have any questions about completing IRS Form 982 properly.

You can also call the IRS and ask questions about filling out the form. They can be quite helpful.

Chapter Five - I got sued!

Well, it happened. You received a summons to appear in court. Maybe the sheriff showed up at your front door and served you legal papers during dinner. Maybe it simply arrived in the mailbox. (Yes, in some states or counties that is how it's done.) Anyway, now you need to know what to do.

It's not a crime to get sued.

First, you don't need to panic. Lawsuits happen. Also, if you owe a lot of money and if you have assets (like a house with equity) it's more likely a creditor will want to pursue collecting the debt and that can mean getting sued. It happens.

So, the question now is, "What do you do about it?" The answer will depend on your circumstances. Here are some questions for you:

Do you have assets?

Do you own a home that has equity? If you had to sell the house right away, would you walk away with a profit? If you would, a creditor would like to have that profit to pay the debt you owe the company. You could be sued and then when you sell the house the creditor will get paid. Of course that might be years from now, but the creditor will need to be paid whenever the house is sold. By that time, you might not receive any profit from selling the home.

Do you have wages?

Are you working? Do you have regular income and do you receive a W-2 at the end of the year? If so, perhaps the creditor thinks they can collect part of your wages for several years to pay off the debt. This is called "garnishment" and is legal in some places but not everywhere.

Can your wages be garnished?

You can call your local courthouse to find out. You can also search online with this question, "wage garnishment by state" or "wage garnishment in (name of your state)" to find out the legality of wage garnishment in your state of residence. There are still a few states where wages cannot be garnished.

Do you owe money to the government?

However, even if wages cannot be garnished, it won't stop the IRS from getting your money if you owe taxes, or the State if you owe child support. Unpaid taxes or child support will be collected by the government by wage garnishment or bank account levy.

Do you want to hire a lawyer or get legal assistance?

Sometimes you can get free or low-cost legal assistance. You can call the courthouse to ask, you can search online for "low-cost legal assistance" or you can utilize an attorney from one of the prepaid legal companies to advise you.

You do not need to hire a lawyer but it can give you peace of mind and it can also help you avoid losing more than you can afford in the courts. Only you can decide what you feel comfortable doing.

Do you feel comfortable telling a judge your side of the story?

If you do, prepare for the court date. Gather your facts. Write them down and review them so you have the dates, names, everything ready at your fingertips. You might feel intimidated when you are standing in front of the judge and there's all this action going on around you – remember, this is *your* court case and you don't want to get distracted. If you have your information written down and right there in front of you, it will be easier to keep focused and make sure you get your point across clearly to the judge.

Can you attend the court case?

If you cannot (can't get off work, or can't travel to the court location) then your best action would be to try to settle the case out of court. That means contacting the attorney or law firm that filed the case, and offer to settle.

Or, you can file an "answer" to the court, and respond why you cannot attend or why you don't feel you owe the debt, or whatever the facts are. Contact the courthouse to find out how to file an answer if you're going to do this. Sometimes it's expensive but some courthouses are inexpensive. Each area is different, so you need to call them to find out.

Can you settle the amount due now?

If you can settle, or work out a payment arrangement, do that instead of going to court.

If you cannot settle, or cannot work out a payment arrangement, or if you feel the lawsuit is ignoring your hardship, you may want to plead your case in court. The judge may be more favorable to your hardship and may order the prosecuting attorney to work out a settlement with you.

What happens if you lose the case?

You may be ordered to pay all the debt to that creditor now. You may be given time to pay it (a "payment arrangement"). You may be able to work out a payment arrangement that you can afford – for example, "$50 per month for two years" to pay a debt. You can suggest this type of arrangement to the court when you appear. You can also offer an arrangement like this to the law firm before the court date, to avoid having to appear in court.

You may have your wages garnished. You may have a lien placed against your home. You may have your bank accounts levied.

Or, you may not have wages, may not own a home, and may not have a bank account. In that case, there's nothing to go after and even if you lose the case, the judgment may just sit there until you own something worth collecting. (If you later get an inheritance, or somehow acquire some property, that old lawsuit can come back to bite you.)

Social Security payments are specially protected.

From the Social Security website at **http://ssa-custhelp.ssa.gov/app/answers/detail/a_id/426/~/gar nishing-social-security-benefits-due-to-a-debt**

Can creditors such as credit card, mortgage or auto loan companies garnish Social Security benefits to pay a debt?

No. If a creditor other than the federal government tries to garnish your Social Security benefits, inform them that such an action violates Section 207 of the Social Security Act (42 U.S.C. 407).

Section 207 bars garnishment of your benefits. It can also be used as a defense if your benefits are incorrectly garnished. Our responsibility for protecting benefits against garnishment, assignments and other legal processes usually ends when the beneficiary is paid. However, once paid, benefits continue to be protected under section 207 of Act as long as they are identifiable as Social Security benefits.

NOTE: Supplemental Security Income payments cannot be levied or garnished. [19]

Notice it states "a creditor other than the federal government." If you owe the federal government it's a different story. In that case, a certain portion of your income is protected, and amounts beyond that can be garnished by the federal government to collect past-due taxes, child support, and some other debts. If you are depending on Social Security to live, be sure to contact the IRS as soon as you start receiving those

---

[19] "Supplemental Security Income" is Social Security's program providing monthly income to people age 65 or older, blind or disabled who have limited income and financial resources.

collection notices they send! Don't wait until they start garnishing! Get into action fast, because you need that money to live!

Chapter Six - How do I know I won't get into debt again?

This is a good time to reflect on the money and debt trials you've recently experienced, and vow never to get into that situation again.

Discover what you may have done to contribute to your indebtedness. Correct that. Here are some common reasons given for debt problems:

Overspending

Spending more than you make.

Buying on credit and hoping you'll be able to keep up the payments.

"Keeping up with the Joneses."

Having to own the latest gadget.

Buying a house without the income to support it.

Did any of these contribute to your debts? If they did, you need to resolve that you won't do those again. It's probably going to be easier now that you've managed to live without credit cards while you're settling with your creditors. You should remain vigilant and watchful that you don't fall into old habits again.

Can you do it? Yes, you can.

Medical Issues

Perhaps your main reason for being over your head in debt is because you (or a family member) had big hospital bills.

Maybe a car accident with no car insurance.

Maybe a heart attack.

Possibly a child or parent with severe illness.

Any of these could have contributed to the debt situation.

How do you prevent something like this from occurring again? Can you prevent it? Does stuff like this "just happen" without anything you can do about it?

You'll need to be the judge of that. You might find there is something you can do to avoid a similar situation in the future. For example, a heart attack could have been brought on by years of lifestyle – you can change your lifestyle. A car accident without car insurance can be avoided by getting car insurance. A child with a severe illness – did something contribute to that, and can it be changed or avoided in the future? It's possible you can, even just a little, avoid having those problems again. Do whatever you can to be more in control of what happens to you.

Family Issues

Separation.

Divorce.

Death.

These are big issues that often come without warning and require extreme efforts to overcome.

How would you make sure you don't have them happen again? Well, that's perhaps unrealistic, since death eventually happens to everyone. Divorce and separation can possibly be avoided by choosing a partner more carefully.

One way to have something catastrophic not be as financially traumatic is to have some savings put away for "just in case" emergencies. That way, you're not going to have the debts (or you'll be able to survive longer without more debts) because you'll have a cushion of money you can fall back on if things get rough.

Work Issues

You got laid off.

You were fired.

Your company went out of business.

The entire industry declined.

These are examples of what many people have had to face in the past few years.

The more competent you are, the easier it will be to find another income opportunity. Also, the more inventive you are with what you can do to earn income, the faster you'll solve this problem. And if you were fired because of anything you did, then of course you should stop doing that! For example, if you were repeatedly late to work then you need to change that and start being on time for your appointments, including your next job. There are often small changes you can make that will ensure you don't run into difficulties at your next place of employment. See what you can do to solve work issues yourself.

Where to find help?

Sometimes you have family who will support you in your determination to stay out of debt. If so, you are blessed and you should allow them to encourage you!

If you have friends who help you (they don't urge you to buy things you can't afford, for example) then cherish that help, too.

Not everyone has these resources. Some people live around others who constantly put them down or criticize all their actions. If that's the case, you can try to ignore the negativity. You can move away. You can get new friends. If you just got through negotiating with collectors, who can be difficult people to deal with when you owe money to them, use some of your hard-won negotiating skills to work out a better environment for your life.

What about purchases?

The plain truth: Save up to buy something and pay cash for it. That is the ultimate solution to debts.

Take pride in your debt-free status.

You have done it! You have gotten out from under the debt monster! Don't forget how awesome an accomplishment that is. Keep that feeling of "good job!" and resolve to stay there.

Daily expenses

Keep track of your daily expenditures. Write everything down so you know how much you spend. If you do this, it will remain easier to spend within your income, and not overspend.

Chapter Seven - CONGRATULATIONS! You did it!

Wow – you are a hero! You slayed your debt dragons and emerged victorious. Well done!

If you know others who have issues with debts, you can help them. You are experienced.

Now, what about the continual offers you receive from credit card companies to get a new credit card? Frankly, they're not trying to help you be debt-free.

To stop getting unsolicited phone calls, go to **www.donotcall.gov** and register your phone number. You no longer need to renew every five years.

To stop getting the mailed credit offers, go to **www.optoutprescreen.com** – you can register for five years or you can opt out permanently. Personally, I like permanently.

To stop getting other mailed advertisements, go to **www.dmachoice.org** and opt out of the direct mail marketing offers.

More information about opting out of these kinds of offers can be found on the FTC's website. Go to **www.ftc.gov/bcp/edu/pubs/consumer/alerts/alt063. shtm** or search the FTC's website for "unsolicited mail" to find the references.

Put those debts to rest forever!

APPENDIX

Helpful websites:

www.ftc.gov – for general "pro consumer" regulations and information

www.optoutprescreen.com – to be removed from unsolicited credit offers

www.dmachoice.org – to be removed from unsolicited mail offers

www.donotcall.gov – to be removed from unsolicited telemarketing calls

www.fool.com – financial advice website

www.dinkytown.net – online free financial calculators

www.irs.gov – to download Form 982 and request tax reduction from debt forgiveness

www.federalreserve.gov – information on credit card minimum payments

www.bankrate.com – free online payment calculators

www.HowToSettleDebtsYourself.com – our website with free tools for anyone

The next pages have examples of letters you can use to send your creditors. Also included are examples to show what you will want to have on your settlement offers or settlement letters.

In the examples, bold text in all caps (**LIKE THIS**) will normally be replaced with your specific information, such as your name, account number, or the name of your creditor.

ALWAYS GET A WRITTEN SETTLEMENT OFFER BEFORE YOU SEND ANY MONEY ON A DEBT.

Also included are the forms mentioned in the book to list all your debts and figure out your budget.

Forms listed here can be found on my website in a special location for you. You can download and use them for your own calculations, and save them for your review whenever you have changes.

http://HowToSettleDebtsYourself.com/forms4u will list all the forms you can download. The username is **htsdybook** and the password is **settle411**. These forms are in PDF format; if you don't have Adobe Reader you will need to download it from **www.adobe.com** and install it on your computer. Older versions of Adobe Reader may not work; use version 9 or later for best results.

The forms in this password-protected website location are for your use as a purchaser of this book and are not for sharing with others.

Creditor Conversation Follow-Up Letter Explaining Hardship

DATE

CREDITOR NAME
CREDITOR MAILING ADDRESS
CREDITOR CITY, STATE, ZIP

Regarding: Account # **YOUR ACCOUNT NUMBER**

Dear Sirs,

This letter is to confirm the telephone conversation I had today with your representative regarding my account.

As I explained, I am unable to continue making monthly payments on my account because **BRIEFLY LIST YOUR HARDSHIP**.

I want to satisfy this debt but am unable to do so at this time. I would appreciate any assistance you can offer.

I am working to resolve my situation as quickly as I can. I hope to have this resolved within **LIST YOUR EXPECTED TIMEFRAME**.

Thank you for your attention to this account.

Best regards,

YOUR NAME
YOUR ADDRESS
YOUR CITY, STATE, ZIP

Creditor Conversation Follow-Up Letter With Written Settlement Offer Request

TODAY'S DATE

CREDITOR NAME
CREDITOR MAILING ADDRESS
CREDITOR CITY, STATE, ZIP

Regarding: Account # **YOUR ACCOUNT NUMBER**

Dear Sirs,

This letter is to confirm the telephone conversation I had today with your representative regarding my account.

As I explained, I am unable to continue making monthly payments on my account because **BRIEFLY LIST YOUR HARDSHIP.**

As we discussed our options your representative offered to settle my account IN FULL upon my payment of **AMOUNT YOU DISCUSSED** by **DATE OF PAYMENT**. I am interested and would like to receive a written settlement offer, on company letterhead, verifying these terms.

In the letter please state the account will be marked "PAID IN FULL" and a zero balance will be reported to the three major credit bureaus, and also that you will cease further collection activity on this account when that settlement payment is made.

You may send the written settlement offer to my address below. Thank you for your attention to this account.

Best regards,

YOUR NAME
YOUR ADDRESS
YOUR CITY, STATE, ZIP

Settlement Letter Offer (sent from your creditor to you)

DATE OF LETTER

CREDITOR NAME
CREDITOR ADDRESS
CREDITOR CITY, STATE, ZIP

REGARDING **ACCOUNT NUMBER**
AMOUNT DUE: **$(AMOUNT THEY SAY YOU OWE)**

Dear **YOUR NAME,**

This letter is an offer to settle the account referenced, amount due **$(AMOUNT THEY SAY YOU OWE)** for **$(LESSER AMOUNT)** if the amount is paid as follows:

Payment #1: **$(PARTIAL AMOUNT)** due **DATE**.
Payment #2: **$(PARTIAL AMOUNT)** due **DATE**.
Payment #3: **$(PARTIAL AMOUNT)** due **DATE**.
Payment #4: **$(PARTIAL AMOUNT)** due **DATE**.

If payments are made as agreed this account will be considered SETTLED IN FULL. If all payments are received by their due dates and payment is not returned for any reason, we will mark this account "PAID – SETTLED" and report that information to the three major credit bureaus.

Send payments to:
CREDITOR MAILING ADDRESS
CITY, STATE, ZIP

And mark **ACCOUNT NUMBER** on the checks.

COLLECTION AGENT

Verification of Debt Letter

DATE

CREDITOR NAME
CREDITOR ADDRESS
CREDITOR CITY, STATE, ZIP

RE: YOUR ACCOUNT NUMBER

Dear Sirs,

I received your request for payment on this alleged debt but I don't agree that I owe this debt.

Please provide verification of debt.

Mail your documentation to:

YOUR MAILING ADDRESS
CITY, STATE, ZIP

In the meantime, please do not continue to collect this disputed debt until proper verification is provided.

Sincerely,

YOUR NAME
YOUR ADDRESS
YOUR CITY, STATE, ZIP

Hardship Letter

TODAY'S DATE

CREDITOR NAME
CREDITOR MAILING ADDRESS
CREDITOR CITY, STATE, ZIP

RE: YOUR ACCOUNT NUMBER

Dear Sirs,

I'm writing to let you know I'm having trouble paying my debts. I am working to resolve this but wanted you to understand my current situation. The reason I'm unable to pay right now is:

ENTER YOUR HARDSHIP INFORMATION. EXAMPLES OF HARDSHIP ARE:
>   LOSS OF JOB
>   WORK HOURS CUT BACK
>   HOSPITAL STAY (SELF)
>   HOSPITAL STAY (FAMILY)
>   CARING FOR FAMILY MEMBER
>   SEPARATION OR DIVORCE
>   DEATH IN FAMILY
>   BUSINESS FAILURE
>   SEVERE ILLNESS OR INJURY WITH INABILITY TO WORK
>   WHATEVER IS YOUR SITUATION – MAKE YOUR OWN STATEMENT
>   OF FACTS

I appreciate your understanding while I'm recovering from this difficult time. I hope to be able to contact you soon with more information.

Sincerely,

YOUR NAME
YOUR ADDRESS
YOUR CITY, STATE ZIP

List of All Debts

- List every debt you owe.
- For "date of debt" enter the latest statement date. If there is no statement (for example, it's a personal loan), enter the date you borrowed the money. For a mortgage, enter when you bought the property; for an auto loan, enter when the loan started.
- For "description" list the name and account number.
- For "total due" enter the current balance due.
- For "notes" make any other comments about the debt.

Date of Debt	Description of Debt	Monthly Payment	Total Due	Notes

Date of Debt	Description of Debt	Monthly Payment	Total Due	Notes
	Totals			

Budget – Income and Expenses – Monthly

- Enter your name and today's date.
- Enter your income sources and any notes. Convert your income to MONTHLY INCOME before entering the amounts. See Chapter One in the book for calculations to make this easier.
- Enter your expenses and any notes. Convert your expenses to MONTHLY EXPENSES before entering the amounts. See Chapter One in the book for calculations to make this easier.
- To calculate your budget, subtract EXPENSES from INCOME. If it's a negative number you are spending more than your income and need to adjust your budget as detailed in the book to balance things out. You can either increase income or reduce expenses, or do both.
- Review your budget as often as you need to get it right.

Income Sources	Monthly Amount	How Often is Income Received? (daily, weekly, monthly, annually)
Wages or Salary		
Overtime		

Income Sources	Monthly Amount	How Often is Income Received? (daily, weekly, monthly, annually)
Commissions		
Tips		
Bonus		
Social Security, Retirement or Pension Income		
Child Support		
Alimony		
Family Income (money from relatives, for example)		
Rental Property Income		
Insurance Settlement		

Income Sources	Monthly Amount	How Often is Income Received? (daily, weekly, monthly, annually)
Yard Sales		
Tax Refund		
Trust or Annuity Income		
Birthday Money		
Holiday Money		
Lottery Winnings		
Other Income		
Total Income		

Expenses	Monthly Amount	How Often is Expense Paid?
Rent		
Mortgage		
Child Support		

Expenses	Monthly Amount	How Often is Expense Paid?
Alimony		
Vehicle Loans		
Credit Card Payments		
Credit Union Loans		
Groceries		
Dining Out		
School Lunches		
Coffee Cafe		
School Tuition		
Education Loans		
Charity		
Vehicle Insurance		
Home or Renter Insurance		

Expenses	Monthly Amount	How Often is Expense Paid?
Life Insurance		
Health Insurance		
Clothing		
Uniforms		
Laundry, Dry Cleaning		
Gasoline		
Telephone, Cell Phones		
Internet		
Cable TV		
Gas, Oil, Coal		
Electric		
Water		
Sewer, Septic		

Expenses	Monthly Amount	How Often is Expense Paid?
Trash		
Other Utilities		
Doctors		
Pharmacy		
Veterinary		
Legal Fees		
Entertainment		
Other Expenses		
Total Expenses		
Income minus Expenses		

Statute of Limitations
20 21 22

State	Promissory Note	Open Account
Alabama	6	3
Alaska	6	6
Arizona	5	3
Arkansas	5	3
California	4	4
Colorado	6	6
Connecticut	6	6
Delaware	6	3
Florida	5	4

---

[20] Source: *March 2011* **bankrate.com** and **nolo.com**.

[21] "Promissory Note" is normally a fixed contract, such as a mortgage or car loan, where there is an exact amount of time for the debt to be repaid.

[22] "Open Account" is for an open-ended contract, and credit cards normally fall in this category.

State	Promissory Note	Open Account
Georgia	6	4
Hawaii	6	6
Idaho	10	4
Illinois	6	5
Indiana	10	6
Iowa	5	5
Kansas	5	3
Kentucky	15	5
Louisiana	10	3
Maine	6	6
Maryland	6	3
Massachusetts	6	6
Michigan	6	6
Minnesota	6	6

State	Promissory Note	Open Account
Mississippi	3	3
Missouri	10	5
Montana	8	5
Nebraska	6	4
Nevada	3	4
New Hampshire	6	3
New Jersey	6	6
New Mexico	6	4
New York	6	6
North Carolina	5	3
North Dakota	6	6
Ohio	15	6
Oklahoma	5	3
Oregon	6	6

State	Promissory Note	Open Account
Pennsylvania	4	6
Rhode Island	10	10
South Carolina	3	3
South Dakota	6	6
Tennessee	6	6
Texas	4	4
Utah	6	4
Vermont	6	6
Virginia	6	3
Washington	6	3
West Virginia	6	5
Wisconsin	10	6
Wyoming	10	8

GLOSSARY

Included in this section are specialized words and commonly-used abbreviations. Most words are defined when first used in the book and you can refer to this list for a summary.

Bankruptcy

Also known as a "discharge of debts," bankruptcy is when you cannot pay your debts and use a legal action to stop your creditors from trying to collect.

There are several kinds of bankruptcy; here is a brief summary of the types you may need:

Bankruptcy Chapter 7 (eliminates all debts except some secured debts, varies by state)

From Wikipedia: "Generally, a trustee will sell most of the debtor's assets to pay off creditors. However, certain assets of the debtor are protected to some extent. For example, Social Security payments, unemployment compensation, and limited values of your equity in a home, car, or truck, household goods and appliances, trade tools, and books are protected. However, these exemptions vary from state to state."

Bankruptcy Chapter 11 (mostly for businesses)

From Wikipedia: "In Chapter 11, the debtor retains ownership and control of its assets and is re-termed a debtor in possession ("DIP"). The debtor in possession runs the day to day operations of the business while creditors and the debtor work with the Bankruptcy Court in order to negotiate and complete a plan."

This type of bankruptcy is a restructuring of your debts so you can remain in business, while paying your creditors back what you owe them.

Bankruptcy Chapter 13 (repayment plan mandated by courts)

From Wikipedia: "In Chapter 13, the debtor retains ownership and possession of all of his or her assets, but must devote some portion of his or her future income to repaying creditors, generally over a period of three to five years. The amount of payment and the period of the repayment plan depend upon a variety of factors, including the value of the debtor's property and the amount of a debtor's income and expenses. Secured creditors may be entitled to greater payment than unsecured creditors."

Similar to Chapter 11 but for individuals, this plan restructures your debts – mandated by the courts – and has you pay them back within three to five years.

Charge-off

When a creditor determines a debt is "uncollectable" or "unlikely to be collected" they can get a tax write-off for the full amount of the debt owed. When their accountants "write off" that bad debt, they call it a "charge off" – this means the creditor is going to get a tax deduction for that bad debt amount.

Simply put, "charge off" is an accounting term that means the debt has become a tax deduction for the creditor, and further collection activity may be tried next.

Collection agency

When an original creditor turns your account over to another (third party) company to collect the debt, that third party is now acting as a debt collector. Those companies are loosely called COLLECTION AGENCIES. This could be a small mom-and-pop company, or a large nationwide company, or even a law firm that specializes in collecting debts. All of them are essentially debt collectors.

Consolidation loan

A loan that pays off all your other debts with that one loan. You may be able to get a loan for a lower interest rate that can be paid monthly for several years.

Debt management plan (credit counseling)

This involves getting your creditor to agree to lower your interest rate and fix the monthly payment, in exchange for the debt being fully paid off within three to five years. Your account will be suspended or closed during this payoff time period.

Debt settlement (debt negotiation)

Set aside money each month (as much as you can) and save it to use for negotiation. Then contact each of your creditors and negotiate a "lump sum" reduced amount in exchange for settlement on the debt. With this method you could pay 10% or 20% of the debt amount and be done, with nothing else due on that debt. Always get a settlement offer in writing from your creditor before sending any money.

FCRA

The FAIR CREDIT REPORTING ACT is designed to protect you from erroneous credit information that may sneak into your credit report.

FDCPA

The FAIR DEBT COLLECTIONS PRACTICES ACT regulates what collectors can or cannot do to collect a debt owed.

Garnishment

To "garnish" means a court orders a third party (such as your employer) to hold back what is owed to you, and pay it to someone else. You are the "garnishee" and the other person who receives the money is the "garnisher" and the entire process is called "garnishment." Could be wages, could be tax refund, could be other income you think you'll be receiving that ends up garnished. In any case, the money doesn't go to you but to your creditor.

Not all states allow wage garnishment, and each state's rules are different. You can search online for the wage garnishment rules in your state. Or, call your local courthouse and find out if garnishment is allowed in your state.

Hardship

The reasons you're not able to pay your debts on time, or have stopped paying your creditors, or think you're going to be unable to pay. Your hardship may have been in the works for a long time or may have been a sudden occurrence (a catastrophic life event such as divorce or hospitalization or job loss).

A hardship is what is preventing you from being able to pay your bills on time or in full. Hardships can change over time, they don't always stay the same.

Insolvency

"INSOLVENCY" is when your income and assets are inadequate to cover your expenses and liabilities. If you can document insolvency the IRS allows a tax break on the forgiven debt amount. Use Form 982 (available on the IRS website) to show insolvency; file with your tax return.

Levy

A "levy" comes about after a court judgment. It is defined as "to seize or attach (property) in accordance with the judgment of a court" (Collins Dictionary). If you get fined for a traffic ticket, for example, the court will "levy a fine" which you will pay.

Lien

A "lien" is someone's right to hold your property to satisfy a debt you owe. They don't take your property, but they have a claim against it so that when you sell, they have to be paid. A common example of a lien is a mortgage. When you sell your house, the mortgage gets paid off first, and you get anything left over.

Original creditor

An ORIGINAL CREDITOR is the firm you borrowed from in the first place, or the company that gave you credit to begin with.

Statute of Limitations

If there has been no activity on a debt for a certain number of years (this varies from state to state) the debt can no longer be collected by the creditor. You still owe the debt, but the creditor cannot continue trying to collect on it. Many states have a limit of three years; a few are eight years or longer.

Stipulated judgment

When you have a court judgment against you, you can still work out a deal with the creditor. For example, if you agree to "pay $100 per month until fully paid" then the creditor won't try to garnish your wages or force you to sell your home or whatever other remedies they could use to collect. This is called a "stipulated judgment" because if you keep to your side of the deal, they have to keep to their side of the deal and not collect. The "stipulated" part means there are rules, and if those are followed, the judgment is put on hold. Sometimes this is your best bet when you want to protect your wages and you can be garnished.

Tools Site

On my website **www.HowToSettleDebtsYourself.com** there is a location for book purchasers where you can download forms for your budget, letters you can use to send to your creditors, and other tools. This information is password-protected.

Special website address:

http://HowToSettleDebtsYourself.com/forms4u

Username: **htsdybook**

Password: **settle411**

Website

Go to **www.HowToSettleDebtsYourself.com** for my blog and a link to purchase this book. You can also contact me through my website.

Acknowledgments

Thank you to everyone who encouraged me – I appreciate your helpfulness!

Callie Giovanni drew the illustrations and gave valuable advice for importing images. I'm so thankful for her assistance clarifying situations in the book.

 The celebrated and incomparable Michael Manoogian (**www.michaelmanoogian.com**) took the photographs. All other content is mine, and any errors or typos are all mine.

About the Author

Many years ago I struggled with overwhelming debt and managed to overcome it, learning valuable lessons along the way.

For the past five years I owned a debt settlement company that helped thousands of people with their debts – all kinds of debts: credit cards, medical bills, second mortgages, payday loans and more.

I've taken my experience and put it into this book to help you get yourself out of debt. I think you can do it yourself! This book will help you learn how.

You can reach me directly via email at **saf@HowToSettleDebtsYourself.com** with any questions and I will be glad to help. You can also send a general inquiry through my website at **www.HowToSettleDebtsYourself.com**.

My Twitter account is **@htsdy**. On YouTube, watch the **htsdy** channel.

I wish you success!

Sandee Ferman

www.ingramcontent.com/pod-product-compliance
Lightning Source LLC
Chambersburg PA
CBHW060605200326
41521CB00007B/671